D0604666

The West

DANA MEACHEN RAU

Children's Press®
An Imprint of Scholastic Inc.
New York   Toronto   London   Auckland   Sydney
Mexico City   New Delhi   Hong Kong
Danbury, Connecticut

Front cover, center: Castle Geyser in Yellowstone National Park
Front cover, top right: Volcano erupting in Hawaii
Front cover, bottom left: Golden Gate Bridge in San Francisco, California

Content Consultant
James Wolfinger, PhD
Associate Professor
DePaul University
Chicago, Illinois

Library of Congress Cataloging-in-Publication Data

Rau, Dana Meachen, 1971–
  The West/by Dana Meachen Rau.
    p. cm.—(A true book)
  Includes bibliographical references and index.
  ISBN-13: 978-0-531-24855-3 (lib. bdg.)   ISBN-10: 0-531-24855-0 (lib. bdg.)
  ISBN-13: 978-0-531-28330-1 (pbk.)   ISBN-10: 0-531-28330-5 (pbk.)
  1. West (U.S.)—Juvenile literature. I. Title. II. Series.
  F591.R27 2012
  978—dc23   2011031699

Find the Truth!

Everything you are about to read is true *except* for one of the sentences on this page.

Which one is **TRUE**?

T or F   California condors are the largest flying birds in North America.

T or F   The Oregon Trail was 100 miles (161 kilometers) long.

Find the answers in this book.

Contents

THE **BIG** TRUTH!

Animals of the West

4

Colorado has beautiful and interesting landforms.

"Inuit" means the people.

CANADA

PACIFIC

Seattle

Olympia

WASHINGTON

River

Columbia

Portland

Salem

OREGON

Coast Ranges

Missouri River

MONTANA

Helena

IDAHO

Boise

ROCKY MOUNTAINS

WYOMING

GREAT

Cheyenne

N
W E
S

NEVADA

Reno

Carson City

Sacramento

Sierra Nevada

Salt Lake City

UTAH

Colorado River

Denver

COLORADO

PLAINS

San Francisco

San Jose

CALIFORNIA

Las Vegas

Colorado
Plateau

Los Angeles

The United States

San Diego

PACIFIC

OCEAN

RUSSIA

Bering
Sea

ALASKA

CANADA

Anchorage

Juneau

Gulf of
Alaska

0 miles 400
0 km 400

0 miles 100
0 km 100

PACIFIC
OCEAN

Honolulu

HAWAII

MEXICO

0 miles 200
0 km 200

LEGEND
⊛ State capitals
● Major cities

The Wide and Wild West

The West includes 11 states. They are Alaska, California, Colorado, Hawaii, Idaho, Montana, Nevada, Oregon, Utah, Washington, and Wyoming. The **continental** West shares its northern border with Canada. The western edge is the Pacific Coast.

Alaska and Hawaii are separate from the continental United States. Alaska borders the northwest corner of Canada. Water surrounds Alaska on three sides. The Hawaiian Islands are more than 2,000 miles (3,220 kilometers) off the coast of California in the Pacific Ocean.

Look at the Land

The West has a variety of natural features. But one common feature is mountains. Some of the most eye-catching are Hawaii's volcanoes. These volcanoes created the Hawaiian Islands.

The Rocky Mountain **range** is the longest in North America. They start in Alaska and stretch down through Canada into the United States. They go as far south as New Mexico.

Melting snow from the Rocky Mountains feeds nearby rivers.

Monument Canyon is a popular destination within Colorado National Monument.

The Continental Divide runs along the Rockies. This dividing line is formed by a series of tall mountain peaks. On either side, rivers flow in different directions. East of the Continental Divide, rivers flow toward the Atlantic Ocean. To the west, they flow westward and empty into the Pacific.

The Coast Ranges line the Pacific Coast. The Cascade Mountains of California sit farther inland. Some other highlands in the West include the Columbia **Plateau** and the Colorado Plateau.

The Great Plains seem to stretch as far as the eye can see.

As many as 60 million American bison once lived on the Great Plains.

Low grasslands east of the Rockies are called the Great Plains. This is a huge region that stretches from western Canada across the central United States and as far south as the Rio Grande.

Lowlands west of the Rockies are called the Basin and Range region. This area is cut through with smaller mountain ranges and flat desert areas called basins.

Climate

There are many different **climates** in the West. Some parts are semi-arid, or very dry. Very little rain falls. Drier desert areas have even less **precipitation**. In mountain areas, the air gets colder the higher you go. The western coast of Washington, Oregon, and upper California has heavy clouds, wet air, and mild temperatures. Lower California has wet winters and dry summers.

Pleasant weather draws many people to live in northwestern cities such as Portland, Oregon.

Many lawns outside desert homes do not have grass, so they need less water.

Southeastern California includes some of the driest places in the country, such as the Mojave Desert. The people who live here have had to adjust. Many communities and individuals work to reduce local water usage. Houses and businesses often have air-conditioning, and many people stay inside during the hottest part of the day.

Alaska is subarctic, with long, cold winters. The ground of the Alaskan tundra is always frozen. Hawaii, on the other hand, has hot temperatures, wet air, and lots of rainfall.

Many plants grow in these different climates. Evergreen forests of ponderosa pines and douglas firs cover much of the region. Cactus, sagebrush, and Joshua trees grow in dry desert areas. Bright flowers and palm trees grow in Hawaii. The coast redwood of California is the tallest tree in the world.

Hawaii's warm weather and beautiful beaches make it a popular vacation spot.

Native Americans in Alaska hunted seals and caught fish to survive in the frozen climate.

CHAPTER 2

History of the West

Native American groups used the land in the West. Near the Arctic, the Inuit and Aleut hunted for food in the snow and ice. Farther south, Native Americans made canoes from evergreen trees. Warmer, southern areas in what is California today provided easy access to food. Polynesians fished from the islands of Hawaii.

Europeans entered the West in the 1500s. Spanish explorers sailing up the coast claimed the area for Spain. In the 1700s, settlers built **missions** to teach their religion to Native Americans.

Mountain Men

In the early 1800s, Meriwether Lewis and William Clark explored a huge land area called the Louisiana Territory. The United States had just purchased the area from France. Lewis and Clark found routes through the rugged Rocky Mountains and reached the Pacific Ocean.

Mountain men worked in these mountains. They trapped beavers and other animals for their fur. They worked for eastern companies who used the fur to make clothing. They also traded goods with the Native Americans.

Mountain men encountered many dangers in the wilderness.

Pioneers packed up covered wagons and traveled west along the Oregon Trail.

Routes Westward

As the United States grew as a nation, people looked for new lands to settle. In the mid-1800s, pioneers in covered wagons traveled across the plains and the Rocky Mountains into the West. The Oregon Trail spanned more than 2,000 miles (3,220 km) between Missouri and the Oregon Territory. The California Trail led farther south. The Mormons, a religious group looking for a safe, new land to settle, took the Mormon Trail into Utah.

The Gold Rush

In the 1840s, the population of California had more Native Americans and settlers from Mexico than American settlers. But everything changed when gold was discovered in 1848. The following year, thousands of "forty-niners" traveled to California to find their fortune. Chinese **immigrants** joined American settlers looking for gold. So did immigrants from Europe, Mexico, and South America.

Gold was later discovered in Colorado, Idaho, Montana, Alaska, and Nevada. Mining towns grew up throughout the West.

Timeline of the West

1542
Spanish explorers sail up the California coast.

1769
The Spanish start building missions in California.

Making a Connection

Railroad tracks soon began to cross the country. In the 1860s, the Central Pacific Railroad started laying track that went east from California. The Union Pacific laid tracks that began in Nebraska and headed west. The lines finally met in Promontory, Utah, in 1869. This transcontinental railroad connected the East with the West. Railroads brought goods and people across the country faster and more easily than ever before.

1848
Gold is discovered in California, and the population of the West grows.

1841–1860
The Oregon Trail serves as the main route west.

1869
The transcontinental railroad connects the western and eastern United States.

Alaska has coastline along both the Pacific and Arctic oceans.

Alaskan settlers built their towns along the coast.

Alaska and Hawaii

The United States found other ways to expand. It purchased Alaska from Russia in 1867. The land was difficult to settle. But it had many natural resources, such as trees and fur-bearing animals. It was also rich with minerals such as gold. Alaska became the 49th state in 1959.

The Hawaiian Islands were a stopping point for ships throughout the 1800s. Settlers also set up missions there. Hawaii became the last state to join the United States in 1959.

Artists and Inventors of the West

Beverly Cleary (1916–) is an award-winning author of books for children, including *Beezus and Ramona*, *The Mouse and the Motorcycle*, and many more. She was born in Oregon.

Beverly Cleary

Gutzon Borglum (1867–1941) was an American sculptor. The Mount Rushmore National Memorial in South Dakota is his most famous carving. He was born in Idaho.

Levi Strauss (1829–1902) was born in Bavaria and came to California during the Gold Rush. He sold strong denim pants to miners. Today, Levi's jeans are sold around the world.

Today, Los Angeles has the second-largest population of any city in the United States.

CHAPTER 3

People of the West

California, Alaska, and Montana are three of the four largest states in terms of land size in the nation. In terms of people, California has the largest population of all the states. But the West also contains the states with the smallest populations: Alaska and Wyoming.

Most people in the West live in or near the cities. Some areas, such as the high mountains or dry deserts, are not suitable for people to live.

San Francisco's Chinatown is popular with tourists from around the world.

A Variety of People

Much of the West's population is made up of people related to European immigrants. During the 1800s, many Chinese came to settle in California to look for gold and to help build railroads. Chinatown in San Francisco has one of the largest groups of Chinese outside of Asia.

California shares a border with Mexico, and many Mexicans have settled in California. The Los Angeles area has the largest Mexican population outside of Mexico.

Native peoples live in the West, too. California has the largest Native American population of any state. **Descendants** of Polynesians who settled the area over a thousand years ago live in Hawaii. Inuit and Aleut make their homes in Alaska. Native Americans continue many of their traditions, languages, and crafts.

The Inuit have lived in Alaska for thousands of years.

About one-third of all Inuit live in Alaska.

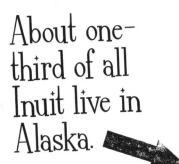

A Variety of Cities

Seattle, Washington, is a major port city. It has easy access to the Pacific because it lies on Puget Sound, a part of the ocean that reaches into the state. The port became an important destination when gold was discovered in Alaska in the 1890s. People could travel by train to Seattle. Then they traveled by boat north to Alaska. Today, many products are **exported** to China, Japan, and other countries from Seattle.

Several of Washington's largest ports lie along Puget Sound.

Fur traders built the first European settlement on Puget Sound in 1833.

Las Vegas, Nevada, is famous for the bright lights of its many casinos and hotels.

Las Vegas, Nevada, is a popular tourist spot. Other major tourist cities in the West are Honolulu, Hawaii, and Los Angeles, California. Tourists also visit mountain regions. Thousands come to Wyoming, Colorado, Utah, and other states to ski and snowboard. In the summer, they come to hike. They also visit Yellowstone National Park to see the park's beautiful geysers. Tourists spend money on hotels, restaurants, and casinos, all of which provide jobs for local people.

Animals of the West

Many animals brave the wild, rugged lands of the West. Polar bears live on the cold, snowy coast and islands of Alaska. A layer of fat and thick, yellow-white fur keeps them warm. Their fur also blends in with the snow. This makes them hard to see while they hunt for seals.

California condors are the largest flying birds in North America. There are very few condors left, however. To save condors, scientists have captured and raised them. Some have been released back into the wild.

Rocky Mountain bighorn sheep live in herds in the Rocky Mountains. Their special hooves help them move easily over the mountains. The males, called rams, fight each other by crashing their large curled horns together.

Northern California's climate makes it perfect for growing grapes.

CHAPTER 4

Resources and Economy

People have traveled to the West in search of wealth for many years. They came to use the region's many resources. In the 1800s, they came looking for gold. Other settlers moved here to farm some of the richest soil in the world. They logged the West's dense forests. They fished in the ocean. More recently, people have moved west to work in the electronics industry. The technologies they build and design keep this region moving into the future.

California's central valley supplies fresh fruits and vegetables to the United States all winter long.

Farming

The Central Valley of California lies between the Coast Ranges and the Sierra Nevada Mountains. It is considered one of the best farming areas in the world. This **fertile** soil produces the most grapes in the United States. Most of the nation's almonds, strawberries, avocados, and many other fruits, vegetables, and nuts come from this area.

Other western states produce crops, too. Idaho grows the most potatoes. Washington is known for its wide variety of apples.

Hawaii is able to grow crops that are not found anywhere else in the United States. Pineapples, bananas, coffee, papayas, and macadamia nuts grow well in Hawaii's very warm, wet climate.

Hawaiian pineapples are harvested and shipped around the world.

Fishing

The seafood industry is important to states on the Pacific Ocean. Salmon are common in the cold northern waters near Washington. California fishers catch squid and crabs that live farther south. Hawaiians catch shellfish that thrive in its warm, tropical waters. Many fish move north during the summer. During this time, Alaska enjoys a short but busy fishing season.

Fishers use special equipment to catch large numbers of crabs and other sea animals.

The western white pine is Idaho's state tree.

Wood is one of the most important natural resources in Idaho.

Mining

The West has many mineral resources, especially in its mountains. Colorado is an important producer of **fossil fuels** such as coal, oil, and natural gas. These fuels provide power to Colorado and other states across the country.

Colorado also produces sand and gravel. These are used in concrete in roads and bridges. It is also used to filter water to make it safe to drink. Sand can be used on roads in winter for better traction on snow and ice.

Computer chips are made from silicon. That's why it's called Silicon Valley.

Computers and Electronics

Silicon Valley lies along California's San Francisco Bay. It is the heart of the nation's electronics production. The valley grew rapidly in the late 20th century when the Internet, personal computers, and other technologies were being developed.

Americans poured into the area to work. Immigrants also came. Today, Silicon Valley has some of the West's wealthiest cities, including San Jose and Palo Alto.

Board Sports

Early Hawaiians surfed on flat wooden boards. Surfers today still ride the ocean waves.

Skateboarding started in California in the 1950s. It was a way for surfers to "surf" on land. Skateboarders compete on ramps, pipes, and other obstacles. Skateboarder Tony Hawk (below) is from San Diego, California.

Snowboarding became popular in the 1980s. Snowboarders do tricks and other events in competitions. The Rocky Mountains have lots of good snowboarding spots. San Diego's Shaun White is a famous snow-boarder and skateboarder.

San Andreas Fault

OR   ID

CALIFORNIA

NV   UT

San
Francisco

N
W   E
S

Pacific
Ocean

Los Angeles

AZ

0   200 KM

0   125 MI

MEXICO

Earthquakes occur
frequently along the
San Andreas Fault.

CHAPTER 5

On the Edge

Earthquakes are very common in the West. The region sits on top of a boundary between two of Earth's plates. Plates are pieces of Earth's **crust**. They are constantly moving and shifting. When they shift against or away from each other, earthquakes happen. The plate boundary that runs down the western edge of North America is the San Andreas Fault. It cuts right through California.

The San Andreas Fault is more than 800 miles (1,300 km) long.

Untamed Land

Many people live in California's cities. They have to deal with regular earthquakes along the San Andreas Fault. Some of these earthquakes have been disastrous. Cities have been shaken and burned to the ground during earthquakes. Repairs can cost billions of dollars. To save lives and dollars, people have learned to adapt to handle earthquakes.

At least 700 people died in the 1906 San Francisco earthquake.

San Francisco experienced another major earthquake in 1989.

People try to be prepared at home, at school, and at work. They have earthquake drills to practice what to do and where to go. Families keep earthquake emergency kits in their homes and cars.

Local officials also prepare for earthquakes. Firefighters and police officers practice what they should do when there is an earthquake. They also teach the public what they can do to keep safe.

Emergency workers are specially trained to deal with earthquakes.

Scientists use tools to monitor fault lines and catch early warning signs of earthquakes, such as sudden changes in the Earth. Engineers design buildings and bridges that remain standing even when the ground is shaking. They also improve existing structures.

Throughout history, people heading to this region had to be ready for the dangers of the untamed West. Westerners today still do what is needed to prepare for the land's challenges. ★

Number of states in the region: 11

Major rivers of the region: Colorado, Columbia

Major mountain ranges of the region: Rocky Mountains, Cascade Range, Coast Ranges, Sierra Nevada

Climate: Semiarid, arid, highland, marine, Mediterranean

Largest cities: Los Angeles, CA; San Diego, CA; San Jose, CA

Products: Oil, natural gas, coal, gold, fruits, vegetables, seafood, livestock, lumber

Borders of the region:

North: Canada

East: Midwest region

South: Mexico and Southwest region

West: Pacific Ocean

Did you find the truth?

T California condors are the largest flying birds in North America.

F The Oregon Trail was 100 miles (161 kilometers) long.

Resources

Books

Blashfield, Jean F. *The California Gold Rush*. Minneapolis: Compass Point Books, 2001.

Domnauer, Teresa. *Westward Expansion*. New York: Children's Press, 2010.

Evans, Clark J. *The Central Pacific Railroad*. New York: Children's Press, 2003.

Jackson, Tom. *The Columbia River*. Milwaukee, WI: Gareth Stevens Publishing, 2004.

King, David C. *The Inuit*. New York: Marshall Cavendish Benchmark, 2008.

Maynard, Charles W. *The Rocky Mountains*. New York: PowerKids Press, 2004.

Rau, Dana Meachen. *North America*. Chanhassen, MN: The Child's World, 2004.

Rosinsky, Natalie M. *California Ranchos*. Minneapolis: Compass Point Books, 2006.

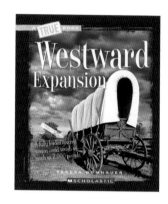

Web Sites

Smithsonian National Museum of American History

http://americanhistory.si.edu/

Check out this site to see exhibits and learn about the growth of America.

U.S. Census 2010 Interactive Population Map

http://2010.census.gov/2010census/popmap

Learn about the populations of the states with this interactive map.

Places to Visit

California State Railroad Museum

125 I Street
Sacramento, CA 95814
(916) 445-6645
www.csrmf.org
See restored historical trains and exhibits about railroading in the West.

Hawaii Volcanoes National Park

PO Box 52
Hawaii National Park, HI 96718-0052
(808) 985-6000
www.nps.gov/havo/index.htm
Learn about volcanoes by seeing them firsthand at this national park.

 Visit this Scholastic web site for more information on the U.S. West:

www.factsfornow.scholastic.com

Important Words

climates (KLYE-mits) — the weather typical of places over a long period of time

continental (kon-tuh-NEN-tuhl) — connected to or part of a continent

crust (KRUHST) — the rocky, outermost layer of Earth

descendants (dih-SEN-duhnts) — a person's children, their children, and so on into the future

exported (ek-SPORT-id) — sent products to another country or region to sell them there

fertile (FUR-tuhl) — land that is good for growing crops and plants

fossil fuels (FAH-suhl FYOOLZ) — coal, oil, or natural gas formed from the remains of prehistoric plants and animals

immigrants (IM-i-gruhntz) — people who move into a new country and settle there

missions (MISH-unz) — churches or other places where missionaries live and work

plateau (pla-TOH) — an area of level ground that is higher than the surrounding area

precipitation (pri-sip-i-TAY-shuhn) — the falling of water from the sky in the form of rain, sleet, hail, or snow

range (RAYNJ) — a group or chain of mountains

Index

Page numbers in **bold** indicate illustrations

About the Author

Dana Meachen Rau is the author of more than 300 books for children. A graduate of Trinity College in Hartford, Connecticut, she has written fiction and nonfiction titles including early readers and books on science, history, cooking, and many other topics that interest her. She especially loves to write books that take her to other places, even when she doesn't have time for a vacation. Dana lives with her family in Burlington, Connecticut. To learn more about her books, please visit *www.danameachenrau.com*.